Red Licorice:
Monologues for Young People

Carole Tippit

Dramaline Publications

Dramaline Publications
36-851 Palm View Road, Rancho Mirage, CA 92270
Phone 619/770-6076 Fax 619/770-4507

Library of Congress Cataloging-in-Publication Data
Tippit, Carole
    Red Licorice: Monologues for Young People / Carole Tippit.
        p. cm.
    ISBN 0-940669-28-5 (acid-free paper) : $7.95
    1. Children's plays. American. 2. Monologues. (1.Monologues.)
    I. Title.
    PS3570.1623R4   1994
    812',54—dc20   94-3655

Cover art, John Sabel

This book is printed on 55# Glatfelter acid-free paper. A paper that meets the requirements of the American Standard of Permanence of paper for printed library material.

CONTENTS

INTRODUCTION

Red Licorice is a series of thirty-one monologues for young people. The scenes may be performed individually or in clusters, such as the suggested grouping included at the end of this collection.

The monologues cover a variety of experiences and emotions from the pre-teener who dreams about owning an unusual pet, to the one who shows affection by making funny faces. They occur both during and after school hours. Some of the monologues are more serious in content and touch upon problems facing young people today, but, in general, they have an optimistic outcome. Their purpose is to give practice in a unique, sometimes complex, form of expression.

Each monologue is a mini-scene in which the player interacts with one or more imagined characters within a specific setting.

If several players wish to perform a cluster of monologues, they may help each other by jumping into the scene with the monologist, assisting with the action, supplying the implied verbal responses, making sound effects or just moving furniture. The choices, of course, are up to the director and the players themselves.

When working on a monologue, it may be helpful to make a rough diagram or floor plan of the scene on paper, marking the places for necessary furniture and props (*see page vi*). This will aid in keeping a clear mental image of the scene.

The setting and props can be kept to a minimum. They can be real or imagined. For example, a table, stool, or trunk can turn into a desk, water fountain, or car, while a pencil makes a handy stand-in for a broom, a fork, or even a baseball bat.

Have fun!

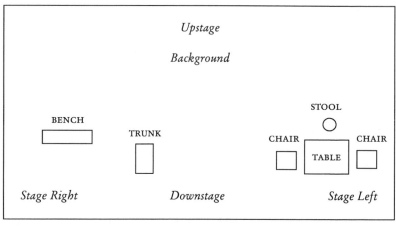

SET LAYOUT

LLAMA LOVER

Setting: A cafeteria

Time: After lunch

First day back from spring break. Jo Jo has returned from his uncle's ranch in Texas. He straddles a chair

JO JO

Red licorice? Cool. I'll trade you my donut. So, listen guys, like I was telling you—my cousin has got the world's greatest pet. He's a llama and his name is Lamarr....I'm getting one just like him, soon as I can.

Yeah...Ole' Lamarr? He stands about—oh, yea high, (*approximately four feet*) and he's got a woolly coat and comes from South America. You can use his wool for blankets and stuff, or you can show him, or hunt with him. What a great companion! And keen senses? Man, they're awesome. I bet he could hear a pin drop a hundred miles away. He's s-o-o-o-o curious and he knows how to protect his territory. Like, he didn't know me when I first showed up at the gate but, right away, zoom! He's in there. Nose to nose. He didn't just sniff me either, man, he vacuumed me, head to toe. I just stood there like this, real quiet, with my hands at my sides, not even breathing. I figured, "Lamarr, if you gotta check me out, do it your way."

He likes affection, too, only don't go running toward him with your arms out or he'll start back-tracking right away from you. He can be friendly like a dog, if he feels like it, but his personality is more like a cat's. I mean, you don't have to dance around, telling him how great he is all the time—like, he doesn't have a lot of self-esteem problems. And—he might not work out too well as a seeing-eye pet because he will lead you only where *he* wants to go, which might make it tough getting on and off elevators—y' know, stuff like that.

Last year, a whole bunch of llama lovers had a convention in Maryland. Thousands of them showed up. Do you believe there are over forty thousand llama lovers in the USA alone? I wish I could have been there. I read where this one lady lost hers. She was real sad. She said, "Losing your llama leaves a large hole in your life." I bet if I lost mine, I'd be real sad too.

They say they're easy to care for and you can pick one up for as little as five hundred bucks. I'm saving up for mine. You guys should too...course, we gotta get a farm first...or a big litter box.

AT THE BEACH

Setting: Beach at water's edge

Time: Late afternoon

Lizzie is angry with her brother for abandoning her to a frightening sea monster.

LIZZIE

I'm *telling*, Richie. (*screams and jumps back*) Quit it. Quit splashing me! You *left* me out there. All *alone*. You and your big friends. It's not funny, Richie. You were all so busy laughing and splashing water in my face and then you just left me, hanging....Nice brother you are!

There I was, minding my own business, just swimming around in this nice little pool the sand bar made, thinking how velvety-smooth the sand felt under my feet and then, Wham! My big toe got caught in this—this trap. It didn't tickle! I picked my foot out of the water and there's this humongous, scary-looking crab with his claw clamped on to my big toe and his other one reaching out to grab—my nose, maybe—it's not funny—and his mean old face all scrunched up with mean little eyes looking at me like I'm some kind of ax murderer or something. So, I yelled, then I shook and shook and shook him good 'til he let go and plunked back into the water with you guys laughing your heads off at me.

(*She gets splashed again.*) I said, quit it, Hog Breath! (*kicks sand in his face*) There! I hope you've got sand in your hair for a week. I'm tellin', Richie. (*turns to go, limping. Stops, hands on her hips.*) And this time, I mean it!

A CASE OF THE FLU

Setting: A bedroom

Time: Late afternoon

Denny sits on the edge of his bed, sipping medicine. Sets it on the nightstand. His mother is in the room.

DENNY

(*Taking a sip.*) Whoa! What is this stuff, rust destroyer? *This* is supposed to make me better? My throat feels like I swallowed a golf ball, my face is falling off, I'm freezing and if I wasn't ready to hurl before, watch out, this stuff'll do it for me.

Did anyone call? Not one? So, I know I'm sick but someone could call me. It's not like I'm contagious through the phone.

What about Richie? When he creamed his knee on the ball court, who called the ambulance? Me! Sat around the hospital with him a whole day. So what if they asked me to leave, we weren't making that much noise. Could he call me? No, he's probably out chasing his little Eileen, baby. And who brought Jo Jo his rotten homework when he had chicken pox? Even shoved all fifty state capitals down his throat. He still can't remember Montpelier. And what about Alice? Her friend said she liked me. Not *like* liked or anything but...be nice to talk to someone....Yeah, but you're my mother....Okay, I'll finish the turpentine. (*Takes a sip but is startled by a noise. Slams down the glass.*) Hey! Something just hit the window. Watch out, maybe it's an attack.

(*He hits floor, crawls to window, jumps up, flattens himself against the wall, and cautiously edges along to peek out, but is propelled back by a second slap at the window.)* Hey! (*He peers out of the window, relaxes into a smile and then laughs.*) H-e-e-e-y! Somebody's out there with a bunch of painted signs. (*He reads slowly.*) "You are doomed!" "Killer germ eating town." "Abandon all hope." "Have a nice day." (*He laughs, gives a "thumbs-up" sign, dances in winning fighter pose, waves and tries to shout to them but descends into coughing fit.*) Richie, Jo Jo, Doug, Pete…those guys are really bad. (*He climbs into bed, and stretches out with a smile.*) Man, it's great to have friends.

NO SMILING, PLEASE

Setting: A bus stop

Time: Early one morning

Lizzie tries to encourage her friend. She is eating a box of raisins.

LIZZIE

Hey, Margaret! Looks like no one else is going to school today. Wouldn't that be a joke? You and me the only ones in the whole school. Well, you don't have to stand way over there, do you? Come here and sit with me. Okay, don't. I don't care if we don't talk. You don't have to tell me a thing if you don't want to. I don't care if you never say another word. I'll still like you and it's nobody's business, anyway. Even if you never smile. *I don't smile much, did you notice that? (She slides over, making room for Margaret on the bench.)*

I remember once, sitting on a bus and this old guy—he kept smiling and talking to me, making faces, trying to get me to smile. He goes, *(she mimics him)* "So, little lady, can't you give us a smile? Cat got your tongue? Your face won't crack. Ha, ha, ha." Then he goes, "Come on, little lady, how come you look so sad?" And I go—I couldn't help myself—I go, "Don't push it, Mister!" Then, he let me alone. So, you don't have to smile around me, unless you really feel like it....I figure we've been friends a long time....Ever since my pen broke. If you hadn't given me your pen that day, I'd have flunked that math test. That's why I like you. And...you fix your hair nice, too. Some day, I wish you'd fix my hair like that....You know,

Margaret, you're never gonna smile or anything 'til you get all your cries out. Your cries are piling up so much inside, you're gonna burst and wash me right away. (*turns to her*) Margaret, is that a tear? You look like...oh, no, you're making me do it, too...(*crying*). That's good Margaret, you're gonna...we're both gonna feel so much better. I...(*reaches into a pocket*) I got a Kleenex. We can share it just like your pen. (*dabs Margaret's tears, then her own.*) See? We both needed to get our cries out. (*wipes her nose, puts Kleenex away*)...Want a raisin?

THE VIKING MAIDEN

Setting: The locker room

Time: After school, preparing for practice

Denny is getting into his gear and handling a football. He talks to his friend, Peter.

DENNY

You know, they've still got Vikings up in Minnesota. Some of them are my cousins' best friends. I mean, they're really fierce. (*Putting on shoulder padding.*) They play football in ten feet of snow. Talk about frostbite? Up there, if you've got all your fingers and toes, they call you a *wuss*. But, at least, you always have a pretty soft playing field, especially after a blizzard. And padding? Who needs it? You're packed into so much clothing all the time, you start feeling like a whale with blubber. (*Picks up his jersey.*) If some guy makes a dive for you, no sweat. He usually slips and falls, then you slip and fall and you both turn into human snowballs, rolling around....(*slips the jersey over his head*) except for this one guy in red. (*Getting into the jersey arm by arm, taking time to adjust it over his shoulder pads as he speaks.*) This guy was serious. Real serious. Had that "killer" look in the eye, know what I mean? Kept making me run, making me slide and then, landing on top of me. (*Picks up the football and handles it.*) Every time I'd make a run for the ball it would slither out of my hands like I'd suddenly grown two hairy bear paws, or something, because of these mega mittens I had to wear. You can't catch anything with them. You just gotta let them hang down with your knuckles dragging like an ape. The funniest thing I did all day was try to punt. I'd have done better juggling the ball on the end of my nose like a seal. I dropped the ball, swung my leg, (*demonstrates*) only both of them flew up in the air. Down I came, rolling, until I disappeared into a snow bank a couple of feet from a frozen pond. (*Puts down the football, and picks up his helmet.*) They took their time about digging me out too, and not before the red dude had punted one nearly sixty feet. By that time, I'd had enough and was ready to crawl back to my aunt's warm kitchen. On the way, "Big Red" comes up, pulls some wet trail mix out of a pocket and says, "Here, eat. You're too skinny." Yeah? Well, thanks a lot! Later, my aunt wraps my hands around two hot chocolate mugs and says, "Take one over to Gail." So, I go back to the group and ask, "Who's Gail?" The one in red whips off her ski mask and says, "Who'd you think?"...S'cuse me? When I give her the cup, I can see that *she* is not a *he*. Gail has her hair done up in braids. All she needs is the metal hat with two horns sticking out and a spear in her hand. She is also laughing her head off. "You looked pretty puny out there, Torgesen. We really gotta toughen you up."

(*He fits the helmet on his head.*) I watched them all tramp back over the playing field on their way home. (*He secures the helmet's chin strap.*) The Viking maiden turned, waved and punted one up over the house. She told me she wanted to be a ballerina. I hope she makes it—but, wow, she sure can kick a football.

I'LL HOLD YOUR HAND

Setting: Lizzie's front porch

Time: After school

Margaret sits in a rocker, lounges on steps, as she waits for Lizzie, who has gone inside to get them a coke. She addresses the audience.

MARGARET

Lizzie just went in to get us a Coke. We always share one before she walks me to the bus. (*She mimics Lizzie.*) "It's okay Margaret, I'll hold your hand." That's the first thing Lizzie ever said to me. It was a couple of years ago when we were both trees in the fourth grade Earth Pageant. We were apple trees and had red paper apples hanging off our branches. We made them ourselves. I didn't ask her but she knew I needed help. It was so dark backstage, I couldn't see where I was going. Lizzie led me to my place out on stage. She had a robin's nest in her tree and I had squirrels in mine and we waved our branches when the wind blew. (*She moves to the steps.*)

Sometimes, I don't like for people to help me too much. Like, they yell in my ear if I don't get what they say, when I only need them to speak a little slower. See, I have a learning disability that began after I was in a car accident when I was five years old. I had a tough time when I first started school because I couldn't hear everything. Even now, if you talk too fast, I don't get all the words. The kids used to get mad at me for not understanding what they said. Some kids thought

I was stuck up, which hurt my feelings so, that I shut up for a l-o-o-o-ng time. Then they would stare at me and talk about me as if I wasn't even there. (*Sits.*)

Well, I'm *always* there to Lizzie. She talks to me a lot because she knows that I'm listening real hard. I like it when people listen. I've learned that some people are afraid to do or say the wrong thing in front of me and I need to make them feel at ease. I like that also and I'm getting better at it. (*Getting up, crossing downstage.*) But I'm not the only one with problems. There are lots of us. Hey, you out there. We're all the same, you know. We laugh like you and cry and we all dream dreams. So, when you see us, don't just stare at us and think we're weird. Stop for a second and say, "Hello." But you may have to wait for an answer.

HELLO, EILEEN

Setting: A classroom during a history lesson

Time: Last period before lunch

Richie sits behind a desk but his mind drifts away from the paper he is writing.

RICHIE

(*He writes, then looks up.*) Let's see. How did it start? I was telling the guys about this really pretty girl I saw on TV, who comes on dancing and says, like, in a guy's voice, how she's too sexy for her shirt. Then she says she's too sexy for her hat and then she's too sexy for—I don't know what—and we're laughing and one of the guys says "Yeah, what a babe!"

Just then, Eileen comes up and I say, "Hi," and she says, (*mimics her*) "Why are you talking to me, I'm not a Babe." Just like that, kinda snippy. S'cuse me? Forget that she had to be standing pretty close listening to every word we said...well, why am I talking to you Eileen?...Of course, I'm not really talking to you. I'm supposed to be writing about Hammurabi's Hanging Gardens, here. (*He writes for a moment.*)

(*He looks up, leans his head on his hand.*) I know you're not a babe, Eileen. Babes are easy to talk to, most of them. Usually. They think they're so wonderful that one is privileged to talk to them. You are not easy to talk to, Eileen. Man, you're practically impossible....(*He writes.*)

First, you've got those eyes....I know, I used to call you Foureyes but I didn't mean to. Some of us may feel that we need something like glass to protect us from them; huge futuristic orbs that glow with a strange, mysterious light; other-planet eyes that study us, ready to suck us up through a straw as if we're the last drop in some weird, alien drink. That's it! (*He gets up.*) I'm a specimen of some sub-culture you're studying. Still, (*sits down behind the desk again*) your eyes are clear, shining and very blue. (*He writes some more, then looks up.*) Then there's your laugh, which almost never happens, but when it does, it's...real. Not a giggle or a snicker, or a sneer. (*Leans back in the chair.*) You laughed at me on the bus the other day and it was really...nice. You usually get mad at everything I say or do but sometimes we laugh at the same things, sort of....My counselor would probably say that's because we are disfunctional in the same areas but I'd like to think that, in about a hundred years or so, maybe we could be friends. I can't say that, of course. You might deck me with the history book or zap me with those bizotic eyes. In fact, I'm thinking of listing them here as the eighth wonder of the world. (*He writes, and puts the pen down slowly, looks up and leans on his elbows.*) So, I guess that I talk to you, Eileen, because... you talk to me...inside.

LOOKIN' FINE

Setting: Susan's room

Time: Early evening

Susan enters, carrying a floppy hat with pins attached and a long piece of fabric slung over her shoulder. She stands in front of a full-length mirror.

SUSAN

Like this hat? It's my big sister's, right? She got tired of it and gave it to me. I'm not proud. I bent the brim this way and that, stuck some cheap pins on it and, voila! (*She slaps it on her head, poses.*) Pretty hot, huh?

(*Deflates.*) But, right now, I feel like a total wipe-out. See, Mom took Laura, that's my big sister, and me shopping today. Shopping. It's their cause in life. But it's spring and Laura, naturally, must acquire massive amounts of rags for all occasions like the Spring Fling, which is semi-formal, and is happening next week. It means that we must stalk every store in town in order to hunt down "the perfect" dress. This takes hours. Mom picks one out, Laura tries it on and stands...and stands...nine years, staring at herself in the mirror. (*She uses fabric to mimic her sister.*) She turns fifty different ways, saying, "We should change the sleeves, or shorten the skirt, or lengthen it, take it in, let it out, try another color," which sends Mom and the salesperson running all over the store, trying to please her. Then, when they think they've found something, there's another long silence with everyone looking on, real hopeful, until Laura says, "I don't think so."

Really, you could throw knives. Now, you know that you're going to pick up and start all over again, someplace else....Only to have her wind up choosing the first dress he tried on, which, if anyone had listened to me, would have happened in the first place. I told her. Honestly, I did. I said, "That's it, Laura," Well, I might have called her "Cheese Head," but as soon as she got into that blue dress, I said, "That's the one. It's perfecto!" But does anyone ever listen to me? Of course not.

Like, I really want to know. When is it going to be my turn? (*She rearranges fabric, poses, studies herself in the mirror.*) Y' know, there was this peach number I tried on when no one was watching? And it looked totally fine on me! (*She flings an end of the fabric over her shoulder.*) I'm serious. (*She exits.*)

PETUNIA PETER

Setting: School yard

Time: Recess

Peter enters, showing Richie his new baseball glove. He may punch it occasionally, to punctuate his feelings.

PETER

Yeah, it's a good mitt. I got it just before I went over to see Martha yesterday. Anyway, she's still sick and I'm feeling weird 'cause I have this new glove and all, but nothing for her. Like, you're supposed to take something to a sick person, right? So, we've got these flowers in the front yard and I pick one, stick it in the front of my shirt and go over. Nobody's home but her and a baby sitter, Mrs. Waller. Whoa! Talk about an old buzz crusher! She makes this face like I'm death fumes and says, (*mimics her*) "What do you want?" She's looking at my flower which is starting to wilt from her evil eye.

Martha seems glad to see me, sort of. We're in the living room with Mrs. Waller sitting in a rocker that squeaks. So, I start telling Martha how Mr. Hendricks brought his pet snake to school and how he fed it a live mouse, which really grosses her out. And you know how real interested Martha is in base-ball gloves, so, I go, "You want some gum?" She goes, "No," but she keeps looking at the flower. She goes, (*mimics her*) "Oh, it's so pretty," and "Pink's my favorite color," stuff like that. And I'm starting to feel like a geek, just sitting there chewing and sniffing 'cause I'm not about to give her that flower in front of the old lady. Then, the old lady goes, "Why, that's a petunia," and then she sort of cackles and goes, "And you're quite a gum chewer, aren't you, boy?" (*He mimics Mrs. Waller's laugh, then suddenly stops and looks surprised.*) And I swallowed it....No, not the gum, the petunia.

Man, was I outta there fast! (*He resumes punching the glove.*) Martha didn't say anything. She waved from the window but she still looked kinda surprised.

VALENTINE'S DAY

Setting: Susan's father's apartment

Time: Late afternoon

Susan has been visiting and is about to leave. She carries her purse.

SUSAN

So long, Dad. See you in two weeks. (*She stops, turns.*) Dad, remember when you asked me if you were still my valentine? I couldn't say anything because I felt so weird. You looked all hurt and everything and I was really sorry but...see, it took all my energy just smiling and being nice around...your new friend. Are you her valentine, too? Anyway, I thought about it a lot. Then, I remembered a valentine I made a long time ago. I guess I forgot to give it to you. The other day I got it out.

It's this big heart made out of construction paper. Really sweet, y' know. It had lace on it, fake lace, of course, it's been around since my eighth birthday party. It had snowflakes on it too, made of tissue paper, little hearts cut out of green ribbon and loads of red sparkle dust. And two little round faces of you and me that I'd cut out of a photograph. Anyhow, it's been in my drawer forever, with that sparkle stuff getting stuck in all my sweaters.

The lace had gotten all bummed up and when I tried to fix it, it just fell off. Well, so much for the lace. The snowflakes, they were from the night you took the whole gang of us caroling, they got yellow from too much paste. A couple of them dropped off. The green ribbon hearts were from a box of candy we bought for Mom but—green hearts? Wrong color. I picked them off as well. Our faces came from a snapshot Laura took of us in front of Harry's Place. We had ice cream there while we waited for her and Mom to finish shopping. Your face is still stuck to the heart but, I don't know, I can't seem to find mine anywhere. See, the poor valentine got all messed up in my drawer—too much stuff thrown on top of it. It's got a bad crease—the sides are coming apart. But, I saved all the pieces (*removes an envelope from her purse*) and put them in this envelope. (*She places the envelope on a table.*) There's your valentine, Dad. (*She exits.*)

WANNABES

Setting: A garage

Time: A rainy day

Jo Jo is helping his cousin, Ben, clean up.

JO JO

(*Sweeping with a broom.*) Hey, Ben. y' know, you ought to talk your dad into sending you to school with me next year. It's not that far, man, you could even ride your bike....Naw, nobody would steal it....Sure, we got gangsters but that's cool. You be nice to them, they'll be nice to you. (*He aims the broom handle like a gun.*) That's the rule....Yeah, I know lots of gangsters. I know one who stole cars. He wasn't even ten, yet. He's got a knife. I don't know what else he's got. I don't ask, man, that's his lifestyle. Let it go. (*Back to sweeping.*) Anyway, why should you worry? You only live a mile away from the police station. (*Picking up junk and tossing it into a trash basket, playing imaginary basketball.*)

In my school, we got a lot of wannabes, too. If you bag on them, they beat you up. In school, wannabes dress like you, they act like you, they even look like you, a little...but you can always tell who they are. You can almost smell 'em, y' know. (*Back to sweeping.*) After school, they run home, put on the baggie stuff and go out cruisin' in their big brother's low-riders, like, (*mimics them mockingly*) "Whoa, man, I'm really rad!"

One day, I saw two wannabes on the corner. They started following me. I thought I recognized one of them but I wasn't sure. (*He leans on the broom.*) Anyway, this one starts saying how I bagged on him. How I said something bad about his mother, y' know. I didn't but these guys were looking to bust me up. Well, I walked fast and they walked faster behind me. Then—quick—I turned and ran at the one guy and bumped him out of the way. He punched me in the chest and the other guy sorta tripped over his own feet and they both went down. So,…I ran. (*Back to sweeping.*)…Yeah, I see that kid in school. I know who he is and he knows I know. He doesn't mess with me, either.…So, Ben, you going to my school next year? They got all kinds of kids there. It'd be fun, man. We don't have to be gangsters or wannabes. We'd just be us.

HOPSCOTCH

Setting: A sidewalk in front of Margaret's house

Time: Saturday afternoon

Margaret is teaching Lizzie how to play her favorite game. It can be actually drawn or imaginary (See diagram overleaf).

MARGARET

You'll see, Lizzie, Hopscotch is really fun. First, you've got to find a really good stone or a lucky piece to toss into the squares. I call mine a "potsie." It must just fit your hand, not too big or too heavy. I found this one at the beach three summers ago when we were all together, Mom, Dad, and me. See? A pure white stone, not too flat, real smooth and round, nearly perfect.

(*She carefully takes aim.*) That was before Mom got so mad at Dad. He said he thought she was just tired of him, I don't know, but they split up at the end of that summer. (*Tosses potsie into square #1.*) See how it lands just right? Doesn't bounce or roll but heavy enough to stay right where you want it. (*She hops over square #1, then hops through the rest of the squares, turns and hops back as she speaks.*) In those days, it was baseball all the time. Baseball was all my mother ever talked about. That was my father's game. (*Now, standing on one foot in square #2, she bends down to retrieve her potsie from square #1 and hops out of the diagram.*) Made it! I didn't step on any lines, either. If you do, it's a miss. That's how it goes. You play one square at a time. Now it would be your turn but I'd better show you. Let's pick a hard one like number four. (*She tosses.*) Yeah! Got it dead center. (*She hops through the squares, returns, bends to retrieve the potsie as before, while she speaks.*) After Mom met Joe, I started getting lots of Wayne Gretsky posters. Joe was nice. Once, he got me Wayne's autograph on a napkin. I've still got it. I'll bet Joe was glad when Gretsky topped Gordie Howe's record. I don't know for sure because my Mom isn't into hockey anymore. And Joe left. (*She bends to retrieve the potsie.*) Now, she's knitting matching sweaters to wear to football games. I've got a birthday coming up next month but I don't think one of the sweaters is for me. It's way too big and anyway, I hate football. I like hopscotch. You can play it alone if you have to.

(*She takes aim.*) You have to be careful not to miss square number eight 'cause it's a long toss. (*She tosses.*) Ye-s-s-s! (*Hops to the eighth square, retrieves and returns as she speaks.*) Some guy named Ed has been calling. He sounds big, y' know. Mom's almost finished the sweaters, so, I guess I'll be meeting him soon. I'm not inviting him to my birthday party. I'd really like to make it to twelve before I have to go through my second divorce. Here, you try, Lizzie. I'll lend you my potsie for a minute but you gotta find one of your very own. And when you do, hang on to it 'cause you might never find another one.

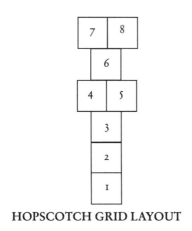

HOPSCOTCH GRID LAYOUT

WE'RE SO SPECIAL

Setting: A bench on the practice field

Time: Late afternoon following a less than enthusiastic base-ball game

Peter expresses a pet peeve.

PETER

Look at us, "The Dweeb Team." We lose and get applauded by adults for *trying*. What did we try? *Not* winning? Half of us didn't show for practice this week and the rest of us are asleep. Still, we got patted on our backs 'cause we're s-o-o-o special. (*He jams his hat back on his head.*)

Everyone is so hung up on the self-esteem thing, it makes me want to throw up. (*Picks up a bat.*) Like this morning, Ms. Sykes asked me to name the parts of speech and I was stuck for an answer. (*Starts making practice swings.*) After class, instead of saying, "Look, Butthead, why don't you crack a book once in a while," she says, " How do you feel, Peter? Are you depressed about something? I mean, how do you feel...inside?" (*Batter-up position, ready to swing at a ball.*) She was "concerned" she said, because, you guessed it, I was so (*Takes a hard swing.*) special. (*Watching the imaginary ball go the distance.*) At least, she didn't send me to my counselor. He tells me how special I am, too. (*Takes more practice swings.*)

When you come in through the front door of the school, what's the first thing you see? A poster with hands clapping and it says, "Let's give ourselves a great big hand!" (*He whips his hat off and slaps his thigh with it.*) What for?

Look, I know that lots of us have good reason to have low self-esteem because no one cares about us. Some of us are even being abused—but telling us how wonderful we are all the time—is that going to help? (*He wipes his brow.*) Most of us have a lot of stuff. I figure if we don't have self-esteem, we haven't done any thing to get it—like me in English class. Like this game.

(*Sets the hat on his head.*) I wish adults would talk to us about things we care about (*takes careful aim*) like…playing ancient Japanese drums, or saving the tiger, or creating our own aerospace designs. (*He swings.*) Important stuff like that. (*Rests the bat on his shoulder.*) Man, if I got started and kept on going—some day—after my drum concert, I could start up my own personal rocket ship and take off for India to visit a new colony of giant Bengal tigers, running free. Now, *that* would be special. (*He remembers his friends.*) 'Course, I'd take you guys with me.

NOT A TOY

Setting: A corner of the school library

Time: First period after lunch

Eileen sits opposite Susan at a table. They are studying. Eileen must be aware of surroundings and try to keep the conversation quiet and discreet but isn't always successful. Needs books, notebooks, etc.

EILEEN

(*Opening a book.*) P-s-s-t! Sue. I've been trying to talk to you all day. I hope you won't get mad at me but....I thought you seemed sort of down this week and....I thought...well, actually, I have to be honest and tell you that....(*She looks around.*) I think I know why. (*She looks down, turns a page.*)

Sue, (*stage whisper*) I heard your big brother's girl got pregnant....No, the whole school doesn't know. Nobody knows. (*She touches her friend's hand.*) I know because your mother told mine. I heard them talking on the phone. See, we had the same thing happen in our family....(*Too loud.*) Yes! (*Lower.*) Yes. My cousin, Jake—Mr. Perfect?—my Mom's favorite nephew? When it happened, I wanted to ask Mom about it but she was so upset I was afraid that if I did ask, she'd think I was...doing it or something. She took it hard. She got frightened and decided she had to protect my every move. It drove me crazy. (*She looks up.*) Yes, Mrs. Connelly. (*She looks down at the book, "studies" it momentarily.*)

She watched me like a hawk. (*She talks fast.*) I couldn't go anywhere alone, not even to Jimmie's to buy gum—I'm serious—and worse of all, I couldn't tell anyone. She went through all my drawers and even listened in on my phone conversations. I'm just telling you in case your mother is clamping down on you the same way. (*She looks down, turns a page.*) See, she may be afraid it'll happen to you....(*She looks around.*) Anyway, I looked at what Jake and his girl had done. I started to ask myself, what did I really think?And I knew that I had to take a stand on it....(*To Sue, earnestly, quickly.*) But, Sue, we have to decide now, before we get older when the pressure starts. We can hear stuff from other kids—guys—that might confuse us, later on.....(*She looks up.*) Yes, Mrs. Connelly, I'm finished studying.

(*She closes the book.*) So, I went to my mother and told her that I agreed with everything she taught me....That we are equipped with something special. We are designed to bring life into the world. And it's not a toy. (*She arranges her books and papers to go.*) I also said that I wouldn't let some guy push me into doing something before I was ready just because I thought he was cute. I think she stopped worrying a little after that. Maybe your mother will ease up on you if you let her know how you stand. Besides, you said you were going to be a chemist.

Oops! There's the bell.

LOUDSPEAKERS

Setting: Doug's room

Time: After school

Doug talks to his friends. He has a framed photograph that he shows them and refers to occasionally. First, he points out his new sound equipment.

DOUG

See my new speakers? they're small but they give an awesome sound. They're a birthday present from my Uncle Jim. He ordered them through this electronics store near the bank where he worked. He was a security officer. Did I tell you—he used to be a cop? (*He walks to a table.*) Yeah, he retired as a sergeant after twenty-three years. (*Picks up a framed picture.*) I got this picture of him in his uniform. See? (*Shows it to each one as he speaks.*) The guys he worked with called him an old-fashioned, sort of neighborhood cop. Like, on his meal breaks, he'd visit the old folks in the nursing homes—knew all their names. If they were getting in a bad way, he'd make sure the people in charge of the homes knew about it and did something to make them feel better. (*He goes to sit, looks at the picture as he speaks.*) At the hospital, he would hold people in his arms, watching them die. He couldn't stand to let anyone die alone.

(*Placing the picture back on table.*) In twenty-three years my uncle never fired his gun to make an arrest, either. (*On his feet, animated.*) Once there was this guy robbing a drugstore? The guy ran straight at him with a gun. They came face to face in the street, the guy pulled his trigger but his gun misfired. My uncle took him out with a right to the jaw. (*He sits.*) He was the type who needed to help people, y' know. And he was always good to us kids, too. He must have been thinking about me when he went back to the store to pick up the speakers for my birthday. That's where he found four guys roughing up the clerk with a gun. He tried to stop them. He was gunned down by one of the robbers—the other three emptied their guns into him as he lay dying....They got away....Now, everybody's offering big rewards, but Uncle Jim is gone. He died alone. My cousin lost his father and I lost a friend. (*He gets up and crosses Downstage.*)

I don't know where they came from and who cares if they are brown, black, white, yellow, or green. They're criminals. They're bad. And they're going free. They're out there stalking us, who are also black, white, brown, yellow, and green. Only we're going down and we're the good guys. When are we gonna wake up? My cousins and me—kids who lost fathers and brothers, sisters...uncles—we're awake now. We're wide awake. (*He walks to the speakers.*) Like I said, these speakers are small but they give off a big sound. I just wish they hadn't cost so much.

APPLE PIE

Setting: Living room of Susan's home

Time: Early evening, before dinner

Susan comes on carrying a tray with something on it, covered with a napkin. Unexpectedly, Arnie approaches. Susan slams the tray down on the table and jumps in front, to hide it.

SUSAN

So, Arnie…uh, wait…I have something to…to show you but first I wanted to tell you…uh, could you sit down?…Y' know, when I first saw you, I saw—like—this early, giant IBM machine…just sort of…*landing* on me. (*Grabs a magazine and turns pages while speaking.*) That's how I thought of you— this big computer nerd with no personality, except for what Mom gave you at parties, that I knew I was going to be stuck with for the rest of my life…instead of my own wonderful, funny Dad. Surely, I kept thinking, Dad will come back to rescue me—any minute now. Only I was too lame to accept the fact that he'd walked out and was never coming back. My handsome, charming Dad. (*She tosses the magazine aside.*) How could I go on without him? How could Mom? (*She paces.*) How could she settle—for you—how could I? No one could replace him, especially not you. Not then. Not ever. And that's how it's been for the last five years.

(*She flops into a chair.*) What a trip! You were always intruding, embarrassing me in front of my friends, with your awful ties and that weird way you whistle when your mind is somewhere else.…And you are always making a big deal out of plain, old, apple pie for dessert, which nobody cares about. When you married Mother, I wanted to jump off a cliff. I wouldn't speak—it was your fault. I stomped around, mouthing off in your face as often as I dared.

And just what did you do? (*She gets up, walks to a table, and stands in front of tray.*) Paid for my braces. Stayed up with me once, when I threw up all night. Saved up for me to go to private school next year. Took me and my girlfriends to Disneyland. Sometimes I'd let my friends bash you for being too strict when you probably saved me from some bad scenes. I know that now.

So, Arnie, I just wanted to say—that is, I want you to know—I mean, I think you should know—that for tonight—I (*speaks very fast, running the words together*)—made-this-apple-pie-all-by-myself-just-for-you—(*takes the object from the tray and whips the cover from it, exposing the pie*) So there!...Thanks, Arnie.

HONDA

Setting: Inside Richie's mother's Honda, parked in front of a store

Time: Afternoon just before hockey practice

Richie's mother is late. Richie and Doug wait impatiently.

RICHIE

Mom and her Honda! She clucks over it like a mother hen— (*Looking Right out of the car window.*) Man, I wish she'd hurry up, we're going to be late for practice—but I wouldn't mind having a little junker to work on someday, like a '65 fastback Mustang. Nah, they're easy to get parts for if you know where to....(*He looks Left.*)

Speaking of Mustangs, isn't that the local babysitter? Sure it is...Mrs. Waller...coming out of the jewelry store. (*He mimics her.*) "I like to tease babies and puppies, babies and puppies—" There she goes...right there with those two guys behind her. Hey! Did you see that?—Those guys just—grabbed her... I'm serious...Two totally baked-looking guys just grabbed Mrs. Waller and shoved her into that blue Jeep up ahead, there....An old lady like that!...Now, they're taking off.

(*He thinks, then he firmly positions himself behind the wheel and starts the car.*) Who knows where they're taking her but I bet it's not home. Hold on. (*He looks behind, then eases the car out.*) Lucky there's no traffic. I don't think they saw us....Sure, I drove before...*once.* My uncle's tractor up at the farm. Well, I can get to the end of the street, at least, to see which way they turn. Shut up! I'm doing it. I'm doing it!

(*Scared, he keeps eyes intent on what is ahead. He snaps orders to Doug.*) Can you see the license plate? I can't go faster. I'm having enough trouble just steering. Wait! In the glove compartment. Mom's cel phone....Find it?...Ye-s-s-s! Call 911. ...Press the SEND button, Lame-o!...Now, tell 'em where we are...Warren Street...Tell them where it happened. Uh, two thin guys, tall, long, blond hair, one's wearing a dark cap.

Tell them they grabbed an old lady....Jeep Cherokee, blue....Can't go too fast or I'll lose control....Can't get close enough to read the plate numbers but...it's a California license—first three letters...I think, are SVL, 4, 6—something....Our vehicle? Uh, '92 black Honda Accord...(*He whispers.*) Don't tell him how old we are!...Okay, uh, Jeep nearing the corner of Warren and 14th, turning right onto 14th, now....He says there's a police car in the area? Have they spotted them?...It's tailing them? Ye-s-s-s-s-s! Okay, Mrs. Waller!...I *am* holding the wheel....I gotta get us back....What? There's a cop car behind us? (*He looks, and loses momentary control of the wheel.*) Whoa! There is a car behind us...honking like crazy....We'd better stop....Okay, let me slo-o-o-o-w down, n-i-i-i-ce a-a-a-nd e-e-e-asy....There.

(*He stops, and turns off the ignition.*) Whew! We made it....What woman? (*He looks behind him, then turns front again with a sick expression. He looks out of the window, Left, with a wave.*) Hi, Mom.

SCIENCE ATTACK

Setting: Classroom

Time: Morning period

Margie enters, carrying books, talking to Jane. They sit. She speaks to Jane, Right; Betty, Left; Ellie, in front of her and to the teacher at the front of the room. With her classmates, her tone is quiet, tyrannical; with her teacher, she assumes a perky innocence.

MARGIE

Jane, I told you, we don't have to sweat this quiz. I saw Ellie after first period. She says she hasn't cracked her science book in a month. Isn't that great?
(She turns sharply Left.) Bag it, Betty! You had your turn last month when she got you out of the math quiz. Maybe, you can do it for the English Lit exam; I hear it's really hard. *(She sits.)* But now, it's our turn....Hi Ellie. Feeling okay, hmmmm? *(She looks up, and spots the teacher.)* Oh, hi, Mrs. Connelly. Uh-oh, here we go. She's passing out the test sheets—Jane, take a chill pill. Ellie is an artist, okay? She doesn't do instant sick. *(She nervously drums her fingers, then whispers.)* Come on, Ellie! *(She suddenly jumps up, looking terrified.)* Oh, Ellie! What is it? Are you okay? *(She waves to the teacher.)* Mrs. Connelly! I think Ellie is having—an attack! *(She nods sympathetically.)* Of course, I'll help you, Ellie. ...And who else? *(Through her teeth.)* Not you Betty!...Mrs. Connelly, Jane and I will help her. Come on, Jane, quick! You get her out and I'll get her stuff. I'm right

behind you. (*She lowers her voice.*) Ellie, stop rolling your eyes like that. It looks disgusting. You're not having a real attack are you? What, Mrs. Connelly? We're helping Ellie. When she—gets—like this—she's just got to get out into the air. Don't worry, we'll take good care of her. We know what to do. (*She starts but is abruptly stopped by the teacher.*) What?...Cheating?—Why—why would I do that? I mean, that's silly. Why would I cheat? Anyway, I can make the test up, right? Now, I gotta help my friend. Oh, sure, I'll think about it.

BRAINIAC

Setting: Hall lockers.

Time: School hours, during change of periods.

Eileen, getting her books, confronts Margie.

EILEEN

(*She slams her locker door.*) Don't lay that "Brainiac" stuff on me, Margie. It won't work. You're *not* getting my homework again. Try doing it yourself, for a change. I really loved the way you and your "sick" friend *acted* your way out of the test, yesterday. Some performance! Maybe, you should try that again today. Maybe, someone will believe you. Your old friends *know* what you're doing, y' know....Do you? We know what *we're* doing too—working hard to get this stuff into our heads because we know we have a future to worry about. But you? You never worry. You work hard bailing out of everything—classes, tests, homework, you name it, and that's what you'll be in a few years, totally out of it. So, if I were you, I'd *worry*! You're getting real good at all the wrong things like—getting airheads like Betty and Ellie and—and *me*—to do stuff for you. Well, you're *not* copying my algebra homework. If you don't understand lowest common denominator, which I think you do, look it up!...I don't care if I don't sit with you and the rest of your little club at lunch. And you can all slice into me any way you want. I'm not helping you cheat!

STONE BRIDGE

Setting: The living room of Richie's home

Time: Saturday afternoon

Richie prepares his grandma for a visit with his friends.

RICHIE

(*Watching out of a window.*) Grandma, you keep rocking and rocking but your eyes never leave me. I can feel them boring right through my back. (*He turns to her.*) When I speak to you, you look away as if you're not listening. Keep giving *me* the creeps if you want, but you've got to be nice to my friends. They're really good guys. Just give them a chance. (*He sits close to her.*) I know you understand me, Grandma, so, I'm going to keep on speaking English. Besides, I'm good at it. My teacher says I'm gifted, that I've got real potential for languages. Why don't you go and ask her? She's said it more than once. (*He goes back to the window.*)

You are happy enough when you need me to speak for you, like when the plumber comes. Oh, then you're real happy—proud, even. I've seen a light come into your eyes. (*He starts to pace.*)

Now, when the guys come, I promise, we're not gonna tear the roof off the house. I'll show them my room and we'll play music but not too loud. You'll see. Then, maybe, I'll shoot a few baskets with them, which can get pretty noisy but that's the nature of the game—and not that I'm just being—"too American." If I speak up, don't say that I'm "being fresh like all American boys," or too spoiled or too this or too that. If I bring home a pizza, it's because I like it, not because I'm "too American." (*He goes to her.*)

I still love everything you cook and the guys will love these cookies you made. You'll see. Maybe this new life isn't so great for you, Grandma, but the old life wasn't so great, either. I feel like I'm standing in a rushing stream. I want to cross but I need a stepping stone to help me make it to the opposite side. I've got to make this big leap, then I realize....I'm the stone. I'm bridging the gap. I've got lots of American friends, Grandma. I'm one of them and—I'm happy about that. Still, you're part of me. Wherever I go, you'll go with me.

(*He jumps up.*) Here they are. Please, Grandma, just give us a little smile?

TALKING TURKEY

Setting: Denny's kitchen

Time: Saturday morning

Denny is trying to have a conversation with his grandfather which he must translate for Doug. The two boys sit at a table opposite the grandfather.

DENNY

Y' know, Doug, Granddad's been doing that every day, almost, since right after his stroke; tearing napkins in half and folding them into piles. We must have five thousand piles of neatly folded napkin halves all over the house....I *know* he looks weird. It kills me to see him like this....So, Gramps, what are you doing there?...Right! He says he's, "Ironing the toast."...Uh, that's nice....I think he just said, "Rasputin."...How do I know what he means? But I got a feeling *he* knows.

He squeezes those little rubber balls to get the feeling back into his hands. Come on, Gramps, get your hands strong again, so we can go wind surfing....Uh, what was that, Gramps?...I don't know what he said, it sounded like— "Boomji." Look at him. He looks so sad when he can't find the words. That's why we keep on talking—talk about anything—(*He looks to Doug for help.*) Ummmm, uhhh...the garden! Yes.

Hey Gramps, remember the wisteria tree? You always said to cut it back before it ate the house. Well, looks like you might be right....Yup....Remember when I helped you plant the daffodils? Stuck my fingers in the dirt to make the holes, remember?...What Gramps? "Gregor?" Hmmmmm....More Russian names. Gregor—Greg—(*jumps up.*) Whoa! The frog! (*He turns, and leans on the table.*) Mac—gregor, Gramps? The frog? The one we saw that day? The day we planted the daffodils?...Doug, doesn't he look—a little brighter?...Ye-s-s-s! Let's see. What else did he say? (*He paces.*) Rasputin...a Russian monk. A monk, Gramps?...You had a dog named, Monkey—something—Monkeyshines! That's it, isn't? Don't cry, Gramps, we're on a roll. Now, I remember. Monkeyshines always shared your morning toast, right? What else did you say?...Boomji. Sounds Indian—sort of. I said something about wind surfing. Boom—sailing! He always promised to teach me about sailing. He used words like, "boom" and "jib"—sailing words, but he had the stroke before he could teach me what they meant. (*He sits at the table, elated.*)

We're gonna do it, Gramps. We're gonna sail. You bet we are. (*He leans back in his chair.*) Awesome! We finally broke through—What's that, Gramps? Uh-huh....(*To Doug.*) He says he wants the keys to the cabbage.

BOX OF MEMORIES

Setting: Margie's Bedroom

Time: Late afternoon

Margie, instead of cleaning her room, directs her friend, Ellie, to do it, while she explains the significance of an old box.

MARGIE

Just hang those blouses all together at the far end of the closet, would you, Ellie? Thanks, you're a pal....What? This old thing? It's just a box. We made them in the third grade and called them, "keepsake boxes." (*Sarcastically.*) Cute, huh? (*She holds it up.*) Actually, I didn't do such a bad job—for a third grader. See? I covered it with gift wrapping from presents I got at my ninth birthday party. It's full of old stuff. Pictures of my dad, plastic fork from the class picnic....That picture? Oh, that's a cutout from *The Wizard of Oz.* See? I'm Dorothy and Eileen's the Witch. She should have been the Witch. She does the greatest witch imitation. (*She jumps up and does it herself.*) "I'll get you, my pretty, and your little dog, too." (*Loud witch laugh.*)

(*She sits.*) Yeah, we go back a long way, all right. (*She puts the box on her lap.*) Look. Here's our first-grade picture. Aren't I the attractive one? "Miss Big Hair." Eileen's missing her two front teeth. She got two quarters from the tooth fairy. She thought that was big money. (*Laughs.*) I got a lot more than that. My old Disneyland button. Eileen's parents took us. (*Holds something in the palm of her hand.*) These—(*sarcastically.*)—precious jewels? These are red, green, and gold studs from a pair of white, plastic boots we shared, Eileen and I. We were really into those boots—lots of fringe—we thought they looked hot but our mothers hated them. Since we wear the same size, we saved up money between us and bought a pair. You should have seen the shoe man's face when we each put one on and hopped out of the store. Of course they fell apart in no time....That's an old crumpled dollar bill from Jane who bet me she could eat a whole plate of brownies in two minutes. Thank goodness, she lost the bet. Let's see, old ticket stubs—and these? (*She laughs.*) These are paper eyes that Eileen drew and pasted on her eyelids so that she wouldn't have to look at me when I recited Marc Antony's oration from Julius Caesar. She was one of the Roman crowd and every time I said "Lend me your ears," she'd laugh....

Just a lot of—stuff. (*She covers the box.*) Eileen and I—We haven't been speaking, lately....Oh, she's gotten so—so preachy. She's always finding fault. She's mad because we faked your asthma attack last week. Personally, I think she's just jealous of our friendship, Ellie...(*She pushes the box away.*) That's okay. I'll put the box away later—or, maybe— I'll just chuck it.

Oh? you have to go home now? Oh, well. I'll see you to-morrow. (*Walks her to the door.*) Thanks for coming. 'Bye. (*Goes to the table and sits. She puts her hands on the box and slides it to her. She picks up the phone and punches in a number and listens.*) Hi. Is Eileen there?...Oh. No—no message. (*She slowly puts the phone down.*)

MR. MANNERS

Setting: The dining room of Doug's home

Time: Early evening, before dinner

Doug has set the table and added a few foods in order to illustrate a lesson in table manners to his two younger brothers.

DOUG

Okay, you guys, we all like Jill. She's a nice lady and if there is a chance that something good just might develop here, we wouldn't want to ruin it for Dad, now would we—stop hitting him, Josh—stop it—(*with a punch*) I said. I don't blame Dad for being nervous—he really wants tomorrow night to be a big success. We're going to do everything we can to help him. Right, guys?...Right.

Okay...Chris, just having your pinky sticking way out like that isn't everything y' know. And Josh, no picking at your food...or anything else, for that matter. Now, we're going to practice, just so this dinner doesn't come off like a tea party for chimps.

Okay, hum, de dum, de dum. Here we are at the table. What's the first thing we do? *No!* We don't fight over the rolls. The very first thing we do is...quit drumming on that glass, Chris...pick up our *napkins*. (*He takes a napkin, and shakes it out, and lays it across his lap.*) No, spread it...don't stick it there. Now, suppose we have a salad...nobody *gives one* that you hate salad, Josh...if we have it, you're eating it Okay, which fork is the salad fork? (*He looks around.*) Yeah, there could be more than one fork. (*He makes an exaggerated move getting the fork.*) Just start from the outside and work in. Not that way, Chris—and it's not a weapon for stamping out peas. And just remember, no rolling your potatoes down to Chris....Okay, I'll tell Dad, no potatoes.

Maybe spaghetti, but no slurping....Well, maybe a *little* quiet slurping...but be careful not to get the noodles stuck in your windpipe....I mean it. Could happen. Chris, quit hitting the table...he is *not* making you do it.

Now, guys, Dad says, "Nothing gross at the table." Ladies do not think it's funny. Like, no chewing with your mouth open, or smacking your lips in time to "Anchors Away"—and the real biggie here, no burp contest when you're done. Now, it'll be my job to pour, so you guys can help me practice. Here are some glasses and two pitchers of tea; one is sweet and the other isn't.

(*Very formal.*) Christopher, would you care for sweet or unsweet tea?...*Un*sweet? You're joking. Okay, *un*sweet it is. (*He pours with great care.*) And Joshua, you would like?... Sweet? Of course. (*Pours.*) Wait 'til I pass it, I said! (*Starts to hand them their glasses.*) Wait. I forgot which pitcher has the sweet tea. (*Sets the glasses down, sticks his finger into a glass, stirs it around, and licks his finger.*) Yeah, that's sweet. Here. (*Hands them their glasses.*) Let's eat.

LUCKY VAMPIRE

Setting: A bench at the bus stop

Time: After school

Margie sits, her books and purse in her lap, checking herself in a small hand mirror.

MARGIE

(*Frustrated, she holds the mirror and fusses with her hair.*) Ugh! I hate my hair! I hate the way I look! But nothing helps. (*She puts the mirror down.*) It never used to matter. I hardly ever bothered to look in a mirror except, maybe, to brush my teeth—But now—(*Looks again.*) Ugh! It gets worse and worse. (*She puts the mirror down.*) Hmmmm...Jen never has to worry about a mirror. Everyone thinks Jen is cool. Mom says I'm lucky to get a new big sister and a father all in one lump...Jen *is* cool. When she first came everyone thought she was at least fifteen. She isn't even fourteen yet and she isn't even as tall as me. All the guys look at her, too. Like, those two from her class who sat on the porch yesterday, staring at her—and sending me for cokes. She just—smiled.

Her father has the same smile. When we all sit down to dinner, he says, "Jen, why don't you play your guitar for Margie," or, "Margie, I hear you're having a hard time with math. Get Jen to help you. She's a whiz. I'm sure Jen will be happy to help in any way she can. Right, Jen?" Then they sit through the rest of the meal, holding hands...with that ...smile. Once he smiled at my mother while tapping the end of his nose, which meant that her nose was shiny. She got right up and powdered it. (*She checks the mirror again.*) Eeeww!

(*Takes a closer look.*) Am I getting a zit on my chin? (*Fussing with her hair again.*) Jen says if I cut my hair, it would bring out my eyes more, and that I should arch my brows. (*Does so at the mirror.*) She knows a lot about stuff like that. (*Looks closely again.*) But it's still the same old me.

    (*She lowers the mirror, as she is struck with a new thought.*) Y' know, when a vampire looks in a mirror, he doesn't see anything because he has no reflection. (*Looking sideways, she slowly raises the mirror—sneaks a quick look—then drops the mirror into her purse with disgust.*) Vampires are lucky!

CRACK IN THE MIRROR

Setting: A bus stop

Time: After school

Eileen stands a few paces from a bench where her friend, Margie, sits staring into a mirror. Eileen calls out to her.

EILEEN

Margie, if you don't get rid of that mirror, I'm going to smash it. You've looked at yourself at least a hundred times. What are you doing, checking to see if you're really there? Why don't you ask me—because I'll tell you—I've known you a long time and—you are very much *there*. Trouble is—*you* don't see you. Lately, every time you look, at yourself, you see—someone else—like—Jen.

(*She moves in closer to the bench.*) You try to talk like her, dress like her—now, you're even trying to copy her hair style. *You're* never going to look like her—or be like her—but that's no reason to just pack up and leave....(*She sits on the bench tentatively.*) You've got a great face. People like your smile. If we didn't have you playing center for the team, we'd be considered just another bunch of fluffballs.And you're smart too. That's why I got so mad at you for copying my homework. *You* don't need to copy anyone....(*She looks front.*) If you're still angry at me for yelling—well, I'm sorry but—I was afraid you wouldn't hear me.

(*She stands.*) It's a nice day. We don't need that dumb old bus. We could walk home...like we used to. (*She starts to go, then stops.*) Why don't you throw away that old mirror. I've got a better one you can borrow.

BY THE WATERS OF BUBBLE GUM

Setting: By the water fountain in the hall.

Time: School is ending

Margaret is standing, books in hand, waiting for her friend, Lizzie. All is well until Jo Jo comes along, making his "blorp" face at her.

MARGARET

This must be the right water fountain. Lizzie said to meet her at the one nearest the art room. Yuck—who left that wad of bubble gum in there? Oh, hi, Doris—Harriet. Yeah, see you guys tomorrow. (*She looks off Right as Jo Jo comes up Left, and makes his "monster" face at her. She reacts with a squeal.*) Jo Jo! (*She turns away, her hands over her eyes.*) You jerk! Will you quit that? You make me sick. Ugh! Just get out of here with your stupid face!

(*To herself.*) Don't look at him, Maybe he'll go away. No, he never *just* goes away. (*Turning slightly to avoid him.*) Pretend he isn't there. As if I didn't have enough. Now, I've got him every time I turn around. Why? Why can't he leave me alone? He goes along, like he's "Joe Cool," but as soon as I look at him he makes that disgusting face. (*She turns.*) He's not going away, either. I can feel him *willing* me to look at him just so he can make that stupid face *again*. He does it in English class, in history class. He even does it during math—how can he learn anything? It isn't as if he doesn't get caught. He *gets* caught—he just doesn't *care*. What a geek!

Once, outside my house, he made that face. How did he even know I was *home* ?...Now, we have staring contests. I stare at him—he stares at me—with that face. Kids try to talk to us—once we walked into a wall and he fell over a chair—even teachers try to break the stare but nothing works. I really liked the time he turned purple—I almost lost it—but luckily, I ducked into the girl's room—(*she tries to cover a laugh*) I refuse to look at him. Lizzie will be here soon. I'll just casually get a drink....(*She bends over a fountain to take a drink but is squirted.*) Jo Jo, you jerk! You got me all wet. (*She turns front.*) Ugh! If I didn't like him, I'd kill him!

BLORP FACE

Setting: History class

Time: Morning

Jo Jo enters, carrying books. His look is innocent, even a little bland. He slides in behind his desk, which faces stage Left., facing the front of class. Margaret sits to his right. His goal is to get her to look at him so that he can make what he calls his "blorp" face for the pleasure of tormenting her.

JO JO

Hey Doug—Denny. Saw you guys boarding down in the park yesterday. (*Thumbs up.*) Cool. (*He sits.*) Where's Margaret? Oh, here she comes. (*He shifts between an inner and outer monologue throughout.*) Hey, Margaret, you're late. Did you know that? You're about five minutes late. (*To himself.*) Keep talking—she has to look at me—has to tell me to shut up. (*Louder.*) Hey, Marge, wassup? Miss your bus? Crowded today? Kinda rainy out—Almost miss your bus?—Get caught in the rain?—You're five minutes late—(*To himself.*)—She's starting to boil—(*louder*)—Right? Right, Margo?—Huh? (*To himself.*) In a minute she's got to look—(*louder*) Margo-reeta? Margo-rama! (*She looks at him, and he makes his face and turns Left, triumphant, snickering as he mimics her voice.*)— "Quit it, pervert!" (*He opens a book, and turns its pages, as Margaret drops her purse.*) Oops! I'll get it. No, let me—let me—(*While bent over, he makes his face, turns innocent at a reprimand from the teacher, and sits up.*)—S'cuse me, Mrs. Connelly?…Oh, I'm prepared for the quiz—French Revolution, Reign of Terror, the whole ball of wax. Yes, Ma'am. (*He*

smiles, pretends to be busy, looking through his book.) Yup.
Ready for the quiz all right. Ready for the quiz, Margo? Huh?
Huh? "Hi-ho, Hi-ho, it's off their heads must go—" Right
Mar?—that big, rusty knife, cha-kinga! (*In gravelly-voiced
glee.*) Blood all over, bloody guillotine—severed heads, grin-
ning, bouncing,—(*Makes his face.*)—(*To himself.*) I knew it.
(*Snickers.*) Grossed her out. (*Louder, looking up.*) What, Mrs.
Connelly? I *am* minding my business.

(*He starts to write. As he does, he slowly lowers his head to
the desk.*) Danton, Robespierre, some French guy...Lala
Fayette...(*In a desperate whisper.*) Psst! Margaret! Please...I
mean it. (*He pretends to go into some sort of fit; eyes rolling,
tongue hanging out.*) Please! A cough drop—anything—
(*about to expire*)—Can't breathe—Help! He—! (*The teacher
catches him making his face.*)...Posing for what, Ma'am? Oh,
that's...er, quite amusing. A whole half hour? After school?
I'm not sure I *can* teach you how to make that face....(*Looks
glum.*) I'll try. (*He sits like a saint, finishes his work, puts down
his pen, and folds his hands. He fakes quiet tears.*) 'Bye—'Bye,
Margaret, I didn't mean to tease—(*sniffling*)—you—are we
still—friends?—Huh? (*He makes his face but receives a smack
to the head from Margaret.*) Ouch! Ooh! (*He rubs his head.
Suddenly he brightens.*) Hey! Maybe she likes me!

GIVE A HAND TO A FRIEND

Setting: The spring semi-formal at Ms. Mozar's Dance Academy for Ladies and Gentlemen

Time: Late afternoon

Doug and Richie stand, side by side, very stiff, in dark suits—formal, down to white gloves. Wearing a fake smile, Doug acts as a check on his more volatile companion. They stay near the refreshment table, watching the dance from a safe distance. Doug's eyes rove the room for a moment, occasionally nodding and waving before he speaks.

DOUG

Shut up, Richie. We can't leave yet. At least, I can't. I'd get grounded for a month. You said you'd stick it out with me to the end and that's not for another twenty minutes. We can just hang here by the punch bowl, okay?...I *know* we look like a couple of snooty waiters. So what? Smile so that Ms. Mozar doesn't nail you....Oh, hi, Alice. (*He follows her with his eyes, nudges Richie.*) She really looks *sweet*, doesn't she? If she comes back, offer her some punch and maybe she'll stop and talk for a while....I don't know what they're playing—sounds like the same song over and over, played in twenty different tempos....Now what? You lost your glove? Where?... Great...It means you can't dance with anyone....Because Ms. Mozar thinks that girls will faint if they touch our sweaty palms....Here comes Eileen. Wow! That dress looks like it has gold in it. And that gold ribbon in her hair! Man, she looks beautiful....No way! I'm not giving you *my* glove. Ouch! (*He reacts to punch in his side.*) Just for that, (*He returns the punch.*) *I'm* gonna ask her to dance myself...pal. (*Steps forward.*) Hi, Eileen. Would you care to—oh, sure—(*Steps back.*) Did you see that? Old "Chuckie-boy" just scarfed her right up. Look at him. His tongue is hanging out....Hey—wait. (*His eyes grow more intense.*) Look at him....No, wait 'til he turns her around again....Look, there! Chuck's got a glove. He's waving it behind her back. He's waving it at you, Richie. He must have seen you drop it....No, butthead. It's a dance. You can't bust him here. Wait a minute. (*He looks Left.*) He's dancing Eileen back to the food table....No! He dumped your glove in the punch bowl. (*Restrains his friend.*) Okay, okay. (*He places his hands behind his back, and removes one glove.*) Take my glove, Richie. You gotta cut in....Here. (*Gives it to him, and replaces his hands behind his back.*) Go for it. (*Keeping his hands behind his back, he nervously watches his friend go. He gets a sudden thought. He brings his gloveless right hand around, and looks at it and looks up in dismay.*) Good luck, Richie. That glove I gave you—as of now, you've got two right hands.

DANCES WITH CRABS

Setting: The spring semi-formal at Ms. Mozar's Dance Academy for Ladies and Gentlemen

Time: Late afternoon

Eileen is dancing with Richie. She is having fun. With Richie, her movements are lively and upbeat but become stiff and slow when dancing with Chuck.

EILEEN

(*Establish dancing for a moment.*) I'll miss coming to these dances next year. I think they're fun, even if they are supposed to be *culturally enhancing.* That means you're not supposed to act like a jerk—(*Does a turn.*)—shoving Chuck as he was about to ask me for another dance. You did that on purpose, Richie. Lucky Ms. Mozar didn't see the way you stomped on his toes. (*Still dancing, she looks off.*) Hmmmmm, wonder why people are crowding around the punch bowl. It looks as if they spiked that stuff with anti-freeze....It's so....(*Look of disgust.*) green. (*Still dancing.*) I really like this music, do you? (*She notices his left hand.*) Hey! What's wrong with your left hand? (*She stops dancing.*) Did you lose your thumb? It looks like you've got a paw for a hand. (*She laughs.*) You really are the "Wolf Man." Good thing Ms. "M" makes you wear gloves....What do you mean, Chuck stole your left one? Why would he—(*She feels a tap on her shoulder, and turns to face Chuck, glumly.*) Oh, hi, Chuck....Um, thanks, I'd love to. (*She looks back over her shoulder.*) See ya, Richie. (*She does a stiff, silent two-step, enduring Chuck's pumping motion to her arm. Suddenly, she winces in pain.*) Oh!...No, no, it was my fault. (*She stops dancing.*) Sometimes my foot gets in the way. Maybe, we could rest a minute. (*An awkward pause.*) Yes, I remember the boys' science project....Right! You got an "A." That's great.

...Let's see, you showed your beetle collection. You had them all—pasted on cardboard—covered with plastic wrap....Oh, I'll bet you have lots more....Yes, I do remember Richie's project. He showed hermit crabs. Brought them back from Florida. The shells were so pretty—(*demonstrates with her fingers*)—little finger-like legs that slipped out and walked the shells away. Kinda weird! Walking hands with shells on their backs....

(*She listens, becoming horrified.*)...What!...(*Looks toward punch bowl.*) Eeewww! That thing in the punch bowl is one of Richie's crabs? Yuck! He's drinking it. Hermit crab punch! (*Realizes that he is putting her on.*) Oh, Chuckie, you haven't seen Richie's glove, have you?

SCHOOL MATES

Setting: The kitchen of Peter's home

Time: Evening

Peter is helping clean up the dishes. He is explaining things to his mother.

PETER

Now, this new program at school, it's good, it's cool, Momma, don't get me wrong, I like it. And you know why? Because it's making you so happy. Like, you've been singing in the morning and dancing around the kitchen table, even though you've been going triple time, working at the restaurant, picking up Julie at the daycare center, cooking for us, buying nice clothes, like, my khaki shirt, man, that's the best. And all that studying, man, you took to it. You pick up every book, Momma, like you own it. Books everywhere. I'm tripping over them. Why, we're gonna need another whole house just to have room to stack these books. (*Moving dishes to shelves.*)...No, I'm not complaining....Exactly. I—I don't want to hurt your feelings because you're a great mom and I know you had a hard time, y' know, having me so young and losing Dad and everything but...well, a lot of moms talk about having to quit school to go to work like you did—and what it was like for them back then—whether they stayed in school or not....But not my mom. No, I've got a mom who knows exactly what school is like right now 'cause we're going there together. (*He goes to a table nearby to collect dirty plates.*) I know there are some mothers in the other grades but—Judy and me?—we're the only kids in the class who have their mothers right there with them. I know—the principal says there'll be more later on but right now, man, I'm the only guy. (*He sets the plates on the sink.*) Now…I don't mind history class, I don't mind art class, I don't mind math—well, I do mind a little 'cause you're picking up algebra faster than me—but that's okay. What gets me is language arts, man. You gotta switch to a morning class or something. I mean, it's either you or me. I don't know if you knew what you were doing last week—when you corrected me twice in front of the whole class.…Everybody heard you. Then, that time we came in the main school entrance together? We just got past the door and you knocked my hat off, yelling, (*He mimics her.*) "No hats indoors!" (*Takes a breath.*) But yesterday? Momma, even if you did catch me with the guys, fooling around in the halls.…Did you have to hit me with your purse?

COME BACK, LITTLE CAESAR

Setting: Front porch

Time: Dusk

Lizzie is seated, cross-legged, on the trunk. She addresses the audience.

LIZZIE

Almost time to go in. I'm watching that cherry tree over there. I always watch it. That's where I first saw Little Caesar, a gray parrot with a bright yellow beak, green eyes and his face outlined with a skinny black stripe. He was framed in new pink blossoms. It was about this time of year, just before the sun went down.

At first, I thought he was a person laughing and I was scared. But when I spotted him, he sort of cooed and cocked his head as if he was glad to see me. Luckily, I was eating a tangerine, so I put a piece of it on a stick and eased it, ever so gently, in his direction. Nice as you please, he hopped on that stick, ate the tangerine, and chatted softly as we started for the house. Then, I almost jumped out of my skin when he flew up and landed on my head. He stayed there 'til I got him inside.

My mom almost had a stroke. She let us keep him but we had to put an ad in the paper first. No one ever claimed him. Mom said that he must have belonged to an older person 'cause he used to sing "Racing with the Moon."

So, he stayed with us. For two beautiful years. (*She rises from the trunk.*)

Then, one day, when we were cleaning his cage, we—that is my brother, Hog Breath, got careless and left the door to his cage open. Suddenly, he flew out and disappeared back into that cherry tree again. (*She walks down a few steps.*) That's why I always watch it around this time, just before the sun goes down. You watch it too. Tell me if you see him.

(*Starts to go. Stops, turns and calls out.*) Okay, Caesar, I'll give you one more chance. (*Waits, listening, then shrugs; turns to go again. She speaks more softly.*)…but if you're a little late, it's okay. G' night. (*She walks Upstage as the lights fade.*)

EXAMPLE OF LINEUP
FOR GROUP PRESENTATION

The action switches from Stage Left to Stage Right to Center Stage. The groups remain on stage unless otherwise indicated. While one group is active, the other must suspend activity and remain motionless.

1. *Llama Lover (page 1)*. The boys are Upstage Left at the table, passing licorice and donuts. Jo Jo is in a chair Left. Denny is in a chair Right. Peter is sitting on a stool Center.
2. *No Smiling, Please (page 6)*. Lizzie and Margaret Enter Down Stage Right. Lizzie sits on the bench.
3. *Petunia Peter (page 16)*. Peter uses a glove; tosses a ball.
4. *Hopscotch (page 22)*. Lizzie watches from the bench as Margaret plays.
5. *The Viking Maiden (page 8)*. Denny demonstrates with a football.
6. *Stone Bridge (page 37)*. Richie, Entering from Left, gets knitting and spectacles from the trunk and gives them to Margaret who sits on the trunk, rocking and knitting as she plays Grandma. Lizzie Exits Right. As Stone Bridge ends, the boys come Down and get Richie and Margaret. All Exit Left.
7. *Lucky Vampire (page 45)*. Margie Enters Right and sits on the bench. Eileen Enters Down Right a beat later and stands with her back to the audience, listening.
8. *Crack in the Mirror (page 47)* Margie and Eileen Exit Right. Ease in music of choice. The girls and boys may become guests at the dance and help out in the following scenes if they choose:

Ease in music of choice. The cast may become guests at the dance and help out in the following scenes if they choose:

9. *Give a Hand to a Friend.* Doug plays Down Left of the trunk.
10. *Dances with Crabs.* Eileen plays Down Right of the trunk.
11. *Hello, Eileen.* Richie is at the table Up Stage Left.
12. *Come Back Little Caesar.* (*Music for a group bow*)

FURNITURE LIST:

Table	Folding chairs, 2
Tall stool	Trunk
Outdoor bench	

PROPERTY LIST:
Red licorice candy—Denny, Peter, and audience
Donuts—Jo Jo
Box of raisins—Lizzie
Kleenex—Lizzie
Mitt and ball—Peter
Small stone (potsie)—Margaret
Football—Denny
Knitting and needles (in the trunk)—Richie
Spectacles—Richie
School books—Margie
Purse—Margie
Hand mirror—Margie
School books—Eileen
Party cups—dance guests
White gloves—Doug, Richie, and Chuck
Pen and paper—Richie (at the table)

ABOUT THE AUTHOR

Carole Tippit studied drama at the Catholic University of America in Washington, D.C., and toured internationally with the university's company, Players, Incorporated. In New York City's Off-Broadway theater, she received critical acclaim for her performances in G. B. Shaw's *The Philanderer* and *You Never Can Tell* and for her portrayal of Electra in Jack Richardson's *The Prodigal*, a role that she originated. She has played a variety of leading parts in classical and contemporary drama as well as musical comedy on stage and television.

She is married to actor Wayne Tippit. For many years, the couple lived in New Jersey with daughters Sarah and Kate and presided over a fluctuating number of dogs, cats, larger rodents and fish.

Before moving to California, Carole was employed by the Bergen County, New Jersey, chapter of the Junior League to direct a traveling children's theater company that brought plays to public schools in and around Bergen County.